Running

Some Science

Dr Andr

Copyright 2015 by Dr Andrew Murray

ISBN: 978-1-326-26117-7

Purple Reign Publications
48 Sainford Crescent
Falkirk, Stirlingshire, FK2 7QF
www.purplereign.co.uk

Running Your Best: some science and medicine

Contents

Introduction

1) – Why do we run? 1
2) Getting faster and fitter versus illness and injury 2

Part 1- Illness prevention and treatment

1) Introduction 3
2) General measures 3
3) Sleep 4
4) Common cold 4
5) The flu (influenza) 5
6) Diarrhoea and vomiting 6
7) Hay fever / Allergic Rhinitis 7
8) When to train and when not to train when ill 7

Part 2- Injury prevention and treatment

1) Introduction 9
2) Injury Prevention 9
3) Commonly injured structures 12
4) Specific injuries 18

Part 3- Nutrition and hydration

1) Introduction 27
2) Hydration specifics 29
3) Nutrition specifics 29

Part 4- Travel and first-aid considerations

1) Introduction 31
2) Before setting off 31
3) Suggested medical travel kit 32
4) Once you arrive to train or race abroad 32
5) Jet lag and sleep 33

Part 5 - The mind game

1) You versus yourself 34
2) Clear focus 34
3) Break it down 35
4) Logic and emotion 36
5) The growth mentality 36

Part 6 - What makes champions

1) Introduction - lessons from East Africa 38
2) Why are the East Africans so fast? 39
3) Lessons from other elite individuals 44
4) What key lessons can we apply? 47

Part 7 - Who can help me achieve my goals?

1) Coach 49
2) Training partners 49
3) Friends and family 49
4) Sports massage 49
5) Physiotherapists 50
6) Doctors - GP's, and Sports and Exercise Medicine 50
7) Sports nutrition 50
8) Strength and conditioning coaches 50
9) Sports science 50
10) Biomechanists 50
11) Sports psychology 50
12) Past masters 51

Part 8 - Your information and records

1) Personal details 52
2) Medications, allergies and supplements 52
3) Illness record 53
4) Injury record 53
5) Vaccinations 53

Resources 54

Acknowledgements 55

Introduction

The crowd are cheering. You are tired and everything hurts, but you can see the finish line. You muster a smile for the finish and, stiff-legged the next day, reflect on what you have achieved, be that your first 5km or a marathon Personal Best. The chances are you are proud of the hard work you have put in to get to the finish but you reflect on a few things you can do next time to get an even better result. What if I had not got ill? What if I had avoided that Achilles injury? Did I eat and drink the right things?

With running, there are some simple medical and scientific things, which, if done consistently, lead to less illness and injury and will lead to better performance. This resource describes the basics of preventing and treating illness and injury, suggests things that can help you run faster and farther, as well as exploring what makes champions.

This booklet also offers information on where to seek help if ill or injured, and a record you can keep of illnesses, injuries, and the treatments and medication you have been given.

1) Why do we run?

When surveyed, people say they run for many different reasons. Amongst the most commonly cited are:

1) For enjoyment
2) For the social and competitive aspect
3) For health reasons

Many runners perhaps underestimate the massive benefit that running confers on health. While enjoyment is not guaranteed every time you lace up your trainers, good science shows that exercise releases endorphins, and other happy hormones that can boost mood and happiness in the short and long term. People who walk or run on a regular basis have been shown to live over seven years longer than the average couch potato, while regular physical activity can reduce the chances of getting many serious medical conditions, as the table below from the Scottish National Health Service shows. In addition, to help prevent major illness, those who exercise regularly have been shown to pick up fewer minor illnesses (such as common colds and flu), and are more productive at work or school.

Risk reduction with regular exercise

Problem / chronic condition	Risk reduction
Early death	30% risk reduction
CVD, stroke	25-30% reduction
Diabetes	30-40% reduction
Hip fractures	36-68% reduction
Colon cancer	30% reduction
Breast cancer	20% reduction
Loss of function	30% reduction
Depression/dementia	20-30% reduction

2) Getting faster & fitter versus illness and injury

Most runners at some point will aspire to get faster and fitter at some point. This is the case whether you are taking the first steps off the couch, or looking towards competing in the Olympic Games. The evidence that habitual exercise is beneficial for health is bombproof, but it is worth exploring how to get the balance right.

If a runner carries on doing what they have done for years, it is not so likely that they will get injured, but also unlikely that performance will improve. Albert Einstein is quoted as saying that "the definition of insanity is to do the same thing over and over again and expect a different result". The balance is in challenging your body with a sufficient stimulus (running faster, for longer, or more often) to lead to ADAPTION/IMPROVEMENT, while ensuring that you don't overcook it, which can lead to illness or injury. This is particularly the case at elite level, where athletes try to induce adaptions leading to optimum performance while treading a fine line in avoiding injury and overtraining.

This resource will avoid getting into the detail of training regimes, as there are many comprehensive and excellent books on the subject, but changes in training should generally be introduced gradually, while listening to your body and acting appropriately, which will help to stimulate helpful adaption (and better performance) and avert excess time spent on the physiotherapist's bed or doctor's surgery.

What this booklet does offer is insight into things additional to your training that can help you achieve your potential and stay fit and healthy. For more on the science of running and adaption the rock star of Sports Science Ross Tucker explains this in simple terms in his book "*The Runner's Body*" which is well worth a read.

Part 1- Illness prevention and treatment

1) Introduction

There are some simple medical and scientific things which, if done consistently, lead to less illness. Much illness is in fact preventable, and something as simple as having the flu can be the difference between a Personal Best (PB) and a Did Not Finish (DNF).

Once illness occurs, following basic guidelines shortens the length of illnesses such as head colds, the flu and diarrhoea. This resource describes the basics of illness prevention and treatment, and offers helpful protocols. In addition to this, sports medicine doctors can advise on possible treatments and anticipated time course to get better.

2) General measures

Paying attention to the big 6 (below) will prevent infection with many of the cold, flu, diarrhoea and vomiting bugs, leaving you to concentrate on your training.

The big 6 of staying well:

- INJECTIONS. Check you are up to date with immunisations, flu jabs etc.

- WATER. If unsure of water quality, drink bottled water; unless you can be 100% sure that the local water is safe to drink. Use the same precautions when brushing teeth and preparing foods. Do not share water bottles.

- FOODS. Eat food from reputable places, and be careful with reheated food. Use separate chopping boards for meat and vegetables. Always wash hands/use hand sanitiser before eating, and after using the toilet. Eating plenty of fresh fruit and vegetables helps boost the immune system.

- SLEEP. Good quality and quantity of sleep improve performance and recovery while poor sleep has a large detrimental effect on the immune system. Prioritise sleep and think about it in your schedule.

- COLDS. These are usually spread from person to person. Avoid people with the flu/ the cold. Wash your hands regularly. Eat citrus fruit and zinc-containing foods when symptoms start.

- TESTS. If you are having repeated illnesses, have your doctor check your ferritin and, if possible, vitamin D levels. Prescribed tablets can replace these if your levels are low, which will boost immune function.

3) *Sleep*

Many world-class athletes are also world-class sleepers. Good quality and quantity of sleep improve performance, decision making, recovery and help-prevent infections. Sleep loss is cumulative and leads to a tendency to fall asleep during the day and a reduction in performance. It's probably most important during and around competition, when travel can make this tricky.

Evidence is clear that poor sleep quality makes it less likely runners will train and race well. Studies have shown that extra sleep does not cause sluggish performance but that immediately after wakening there is a period of about 90 minutes when performance would be reduced if you tried to run.

Recommendations
- Individuals vary but ideally aim for close to 8 hours or more
- Avoid competing within 90 minutes of waking up from deep sleep
- Consider sleep as part of your training and prioritise it
- Get into a regular routine- sleep is trainable
- Avoid stimulants (caffeine and alcohol) and big meals prior to bed
- Warm baths-neither too hot nor too cold- can aid sleep
- Plan and prioritise sleep when travelling paying attention to flights, hotels, packing ear plugs, eye shields etc.
- Inability to sleep well is sometimes a symptom of over-training

4) *Common cold*

Headcolds are usually caused by a viral illness. Symptoms include cough, sneezing, nasal discharge and headaches. The body itself will fight off a cold, but the duration of illness can be shortened by about a day by doing a few basic things. If during important competition, or if a cold lasts more than a week, check in with your doctor to check your symptoms are not due to a bacterial infection, allergy, or other cause. Prevention of colds and flu includes minimising contact with anyone with symptoms. Prevent spread to others by not sharing drinks, cough into a tissue, and wash your hands regularly.

Recommendations
- Prevent colds/ viral upper respiratory illness by using First Defence spray prior to flights, or when in contact with family and friends who are ill.

- If symptoms have lasted more than a week see a doctor to ensure it is nothing more serious.
- Eating and sleeping well helps prevent these illnesses in the first place while eating/ drinking citrus fruit, fresh fruit and vegetables and ensuring good quality and quantity of sleep shortens the length of illness.
- Vitamin C and zinc can shorten these illnesses. When symptoms start, drink 2 glasses of fresh orange per day and consider using zinc lozenges.
- If symptoms above the neck only, such as blocked or runny nose and mild sore throat, then training should do you no harm
- If symptoms below the neck such as chest congestion, dirty cough, aching bones or muscles, fever, shivering or chills, or pus on throat then if practical take the day off training as exercise can make the symptoms worse.
- Paracetamol (acetaminophen) can help with pain and mild fever. If you are a professional athlete check with a doctor prior to taking any other flu remedy as some contain pseudoephedrine which is currently banned for competitions that feature drug testing and is commonly found in over the counter cold remedies.

5) *The flu (influenza)*

Flu (Influenza) is a more serious viral infection that sometimes occurs at random, but also occurs in epidemics, spreading rapidly and infecting large numbers of people. The symptoms of flu include those similar to a cold but are more severe and in addition to sneezing, nasal congestion/ runniness, cough and mild headaches usually include muscle and joint aching, fever and severe fatigue. Sometimes the flu can make you more likely to also to develop a bacterial chest infection.

If during important competition, or if symptoms are slow to resolve, check in with medical staff to ensure your symptoms are not due to bacterial infection, or other cause. Prevention of flu includes minimising contact with anyone with symptoms. Prevent spreading flu or common colds to others by not sharing drinks, and do cough into a tissue (not your hand), and wash your hands regularly.

Recommendations

- Get your flu vaccine every year. This can prevent about 60% of flu-like illness. In the Northern hemisphere these are usually best given in late September/ October
- Prevent colds/ viral upper respiratory illness by using First Defence spray prior to flights, or when in contact with family and friends who are ill

- Consider seeing a doctor if illness slow to resolve to ensure it is nothing more serious, and for advice on getting better quicker
- Eating and sleeping well helps prevent these illnesses in the first place while eating/ drinking citrus fruit, fresh fruit and vegetables and ensuring good quality and quantity of sleep shortens the length of illness.
- Vitamin C and zinc can shorten these illnesses, drink 2 glasses of fresh orange per day and use zinc lozenges when symptoms start.
- If symptoms above the neck only such as blocked or runny nose, and mild sore throat then training should do you no harm
- Paracetamol (acetaminophen) can help with pain and mild fever.
- After a bad flu illness, ease yourself back into exercise gradually

6) Diarrhoea and vomiting

The most frequent causes of diarrhoea and vomiting are gut infections. These can be due to viruses, bacteria or parasites. Attention to a few basics prevents most infections occurring.

Prevention
- If you are not sure if the water is "drinkable" locally, use bottled water to drink, clean teeth, wash fruit and vegetables etc.
- Avoid sharing drinks, or finger food with other people
- Wash your hands properly (or use hand sanitiser) before eating, and after going to the toilet.
- Avoid foods that you think might be "dodgy"- your gut instinct is often right! Consider avoiding barbeque food, street food, reheated rice etc unless you are sure it has been prepared cleanly.
- Avoid contact with those that have active diarrhoea and/ or vomiting.
- Stay up to date each year with your immunisations.

Treatment

- The treatment of diarrhoea and vomiting depends upon where you are. Different countries have different causes. It is often wise to speak to, or see a doctor. Definitely see a doctor if there is blood or slime in your diarrhoea or vomit.
- Drink small amounts of non-carbonated, non-alcoholic drinks often to stay hydrated- try and keep your pee either clear, or straw-coloured.
- Imodium/ Loperamide can decrease the frequency of needing to go to the toilet- useful if travelling, but diarrhoea can be nature's way of flushing out the bugs so it may be wise to hold off. It is worth having Loperamide/ Imodium in your medical kit.
- Probiotics like Yakult or Actimel can replenish the gut's good bacteria- take 2-3 per day if you have diarrhoea.

- Other treatments depend on your schedule and geographical location.

7) *Hay fever / Allergic Rhinitis*

Hay fever affects runners, particularly in the spring and summer. It is usually an allergic condition, often to grass or other plant pollen. The medical term is "seasonal allergic rhinitis". Some people get hay fever like symptoms when exposed to other "triggers" of which animal fur is a common trigger.

Common symptoms include.
- Runny nose
- Sneezing
- Itch, either generally, or around the eyes.

Treatments depend on which symptoms are the most troublesome. Treatments can either be general hay fever treatments, or target specific symptoms. Work out what likely triggers your hay fever and avoid this trigger as much as possible

- Antihistamine tablets generally are of two types.
- Sedating antihistamines (like Piriton, chlorpheniramine etc) decrease itch and other symptoms but cause some sleepiness. These can be taken to counter itch at night, but the sleepiness won't help your driving or running.
- Non-sedating antihistamines (for example cetirizine, loratadine) are slightly less powerful against hay fever symptoms but do generally work well and do not cause sleepiness or sedation.
- If you have mostly nasal symptoms, a corticosteroid nasal spray prescribed by your doctor may help.
- Itch and watery eyes can be improved by eye drops, such as sodium chromoglycate drops.
- Many treatments do not require a prescription and can be bought from the chemist, but a doctor may help target treatment appropriately.

8) *When to train and when not to train when ill*

Sometimes when you are ill it is safe to train. At other times it will harm your health or potentially pass bugs on to others. Please do not exercise heavily (run/ go to gym) if ANY of the following apply- if they don't apply you can probably train.

Problem	Advice
Diarrhoea	stay at home- often contagious- follow diarrhoea treatment advice
Vomiting	stay at home- often contagious
Fever	Avoid training and establish cause
Bringing stuff up when you cough	Request review with doctor
Pus on tonsils	Request review with doctor
Resting pulse/ heart rate is over 80	if resting pulse over 80 do not train if resting pulse over 74 do not do a heavy session
Severe muscle aches	Avoid using very sore muscle groups

Simple head colds/ viruses are unlikely to stop you training.

Part 2- Injury prevention and treatment

1) Introduction

Around 80% of runners will suffer at least one injury per year, but it doesn't have to be this way.

Some basic knowledge of injury prevention, the structures of the human body, the potential cause of the injury and how to treat it are invaluable in staying injury-free, and sorting out any problems when they do occur. Many studies have looked at injuries in runners, and the good news is that most injuries can be predicted and avoided. Although prevention is better than cure, when injuries do occur, an accurate diagnosis ensures rapid and effective treatment.

2) Injury prevention

Most injuries in some sports are "acute" injures- i.e. caused by a particular event/ sudden force at one point in time (for example a cruciate ligament injury in a footballer), while the vast majority of running injuries are "overuse" in nature. The good news about overuse injuries is that they are generally predictable and preventable. It is often not necessary to stop running.

Most people would consider jumping out of an aeroplane without a parachute to be foolish. An injury is very likely to occur. Putting protective factors in place like a parachute, and perhaps a helmet and an experienced instructor, would seem wise. It is perhaps less obvious, but there are common errors which will almost always lead to injury and misery in runners. Although your injuries are less dramatic than those sustained by the non-parachuted jumper, the misery of being cooped up with an injury is difficult to underestimate.

Most injuries can be attributed to one of four factors

1) Too quick an increase in training volume (i.e. increasing the total number of miles run each week by more than 10-12% per week)

2) Too quick an increase in intensity or alteration in type of training (i.e rapidly increasing the speed at which you are running or changing to very hilly terrain)

3) Biomechanical errors (the way your body moves, and the forces being exerted on different parts of the body)

4) Not listening to your body when an injury occurs

A rapid increase in training volume is an extremely common cause of injury. When training for a particular event, allowing enough weeks for adequate preparation and training will help avoid this scenario. Although people are different, increasing training volume by no more than 5 miles per week, or 10% (whichever is more) will massively decrease the chance of ending up on the physiotherapist's couch.

Overuse/ overload injuries are due to cumulative force upon a particular part of the body, so even if you have not increased the amount you are doing, increasing the intensity (or how fast you run) suddenly can have a similar effect. Likewise, changing to different terrain (ie hilly, hard or uneven surfaces, running only on one side of the camber) can place stress upon the body. The key message is to introduce change gradually.

Sometimes even if you do not increase the volume or intensity of running, injury can occur. This is more likely if you have abnormal biomechanical factors. Biomechanics in simple terms is how your body moves and how force is exerted on your body when you move. Biomechanics are affected by intrinsic (your body) factors, and extrinsic (external) factors. Some biomechanical factors that predispose to injury are listed below (there are many others).

Extrinsic factors	Intrinsic factors
Inappropriate footwear Sudden change in footwear Sudden change in terrain Running on one side of the camber all the time	Muscle imbalance Poor gluteal (bum muscle) control Poor foot position on landing Overstriding Excessive horizontal / side to side movement Excessive up and down movement (vertical displacement) Hyperpronation or oversupination

Usually a runner can figure out the extrinsic factors themselves, while a coach, running shop with video analysis or physio can point out obvious intrinsic problems. Simply because one of these applies does not necessarily mean you will get injured, but the more risk factors you have, especially when you are changing/ increasing your training mean that injury is more likely. As a crude analogy, if a team has no bad footballers, they are likely to do well. The more bad components/ players they have, the poorer the performance of the team is likely to be. If most of the team are duffers, or there are some very bad performers then changes need to be made otherwise the results will be terrible. With runners, the more biomechanical faults there are, and the worse these faults are, the more likely an injury will occur. Avoiding them in the first place, or correcting them when they happen, will keep you on track.

If an overuse injury is developing, then unless you change something in terms of the amount or intensity you are running, or address a biomechanical factor, it will probably just get worse and worse. Listen to your body- even minor alterations can make a significant difference.

Some other basics

Running coaches can be helpful in giving advice on training and technique that can decrease the likelihood of an injury occurring and can help resolve an injury if it occurs, helping to make you faster. Often the first thing we do as amateur sportsmen and women when results are not going our way is to buy more fancy equipment like a new tennis racquet or golf clubs or running shoes when actually advice on technique can help get better results.

Although many will tell you otherwise, there is no evidence that stretching before a run makes injury less likely. What can help is a gradual build-up of pace for a couple of minutes, or a warm-up jog prior to a race. Stretching after exercise can decrease the chance of injury. The key is to stretch off each large muscle group and 5 minutes stretching after a run is time well used. This can even be done in front of the television! But again, take advice as to the best form of stretching to do, and how to do it.

Certain types of shoe are better for certain people. If you have found a particular type that is comfortable and works for you- buy some more! A good running shop may help you select a pair that suits you. Throw your shoes away after 500 miles maximum. They will have lost most of their shock-absorbing ability and make injury more likely.

Top tips for injury prevention
- **If an injury is developing try and work out what's causing it and change the problem**
- **Avoid increasing volume (distance you run) too quickly**
- **Avoid increasing the intensity (speed you run) too quickly**
- **Avoid suddenly switching to hilly or uneven terrain**
- **Consider if your shoes are right for you and if you change, swap over gradually**
- **Throw shoes out after 500 miles maximum**
- **Stretch after you run**
- **Start gradually for the first 2 minutes**
- **Consider your biomechanics- get this checked if you are often injured**
- **Listen to your body and go back to an amount of running you know was ok**
- **If you develop a sudden problem see an expert (physio/ GP/ sports doctor**
- **Expert help from a running coach, sports doctor, physio, osteopath is often money well spent**

3) Commonly injured structures

The musculoskeletal system is made up of a number of different types of structure/ tissues. Some types of structures are more commonly injured in runners than others. In general injuries below the waist are more common due to the repeated forces placed upon the legs when running.

The table below shows some common running injuries (there are many others)

"overuse/ overload"	"acute"
Blisters Chafing Delayed Onset Muscle Soreness (DOMS). Achilles tendinopathy Iliotibial band syndrome Front of knee pain (often caused by patellofemoral syndrome, or patella tendinopathy) Shin splints (Medial Tibial Stress Syndrome) Stress fractures (foot, leg, pelvis) Osteoarthritis (wear and tear arthritis) Plantar Fasciitis Groin pain	Ankle sprains Muscle strain/ tear (calf, hamstring most common) Cuts/ grazes/ bruises

Bones

Bones help support and protect the other parts of the body, in addition to producing blood cells, and storing minerals. They help produce leverage and movement. They are strong, are hard to the touch, and come in a variety of shapes and sizes. There are 206 bones in the adult human body.

Bones are usually damaged either from a sudden or severe force causing "fracture" (break), or from much smaller but repetitive forces causing "stress reaction" or "stress fracture", or due to a medical condition that causes inappropriate weakening of the bone.

Whilst most bone injuries in contact sports are acute (usually caused by a sudden, massive force), most bone injuries in runners are repeated and smaller forces as the foot hits the ground, with every stride causing overuse injuries of bone. When the repetitive forces are bigger than the body's ability to repair itself, a stress fracture results. Common places for these to occur are in the foot and shins. These injuries will be discussed in the chapter on stress fractures. Unlike many other structures, injuries to bone generally require time to heal, and usually require time off running (perhaps doing some cycling or swimming meantime).

Tendons

Tendons connect muscle to bone, working with muscle to move bone. They are made of connective tissue helping transmit force, store and recycle elastic energy and withstand tension. The length and size of a tendon varies greatly between people- this affects athletic ability, and susceptibility to injury. The kangaroo has massive achilles tendons, contributing to its elastic hopping movements. The achilles tendon is the largest in the human body, connecting the heel bone to the calf muscle and is also the most commonly injured.

Essentially, your tendons are like your most boring friend. They just want to do the same thing over and over again and this keeps them happy. As soon as you do something very different (like suddenly increasing the amount or the speed that you run, or altering the way that you run, perhaps by using different footwear) at least one of your tendons is likely to complain. The most cantankerous are usually the achilles tendon, or the patella tendon (which connects your knee cap to your tibia) and these tendons are often the first to grumble.

Sometimes acute (sudden) injuries occur. An example is a completely ruptured (broken) achilles tendon. Completely ruptured tendons often require surgery to fix them, or at least a plastercast to hold the tendon in position to allow healing. Smaller tears can occur, when part of the tendon is broken. However, well over 90% of tendon injuries in runners are overuse, chronic injuries causing pain, and often swelling at a point of the tendon but without tearing, or with only very small tears. It is almost always possible to establish a cause for these injuries, which helps prevent them coming back once the problem is fixed.

Tendon pain is usually directly over a tendon and is sore to pinch. Typically it is sore and swollen first thing in the morning and when you start running but the pain is bearable and it eases off a bit when you run. It then becomes painful again after stopping. When seen before the problem has been going on for too long, a "reactive" tendon is described. Essentially the tendon is swollen, sore and complaining but can usually be settled with various treatments as described later. If it has been going on for some time doctors and physios might describe a "degenerative" tendon, meaning there is wear and tear and it will take longer to get the problem better. A degenerative tendon is at a higher risk of breaking completely or "rupturing".

Treatment of overuse tendon injuries depends on which tendon is affected, and how bad it is, but often the POLICE approach is tried in the first instance

Protect from further injury and avoid carrying on doing the things that have caused the injury which may involve temporarily cutting back, but not stopping, the amount of running you do.

Optimise **L**oad. There is a certain amount and types of exercise that benefits these tendons. A physio will be able to guide you with this.

Ice. Apply ice to the sore area for 10 minutes twice a day.

Clever stuff. Certain medications from a sports doctor can help.

Elevation. The swelling can be taken away from the tendon by having the affected bit above the level of your heart (for example put a pillow under your legs when sleeping).

If your tendon is still grumbling despite physio and the above, it can be useful to see a sports doctor to establish a clear diagnosis, and consider fancier treatments. Tendons are not seen well on X-ray but are seen beautifully on ultrasound, or MRI and issues are diagnosed in this way if it is not obvious from examination. However, most of the time your physio or sports doctor will offer appropriate rehab and advice without needing these scans. There are various medications and injections that can be used in specific conditions. For example, new evidence shows that Ibuprofen (either as a cream or in tablet form) can be helpful for grumpy tendons or "tendinosis", although other anti-inflammatories are not helpful.

Muscles

The human body also has heart (cardiac) and bowel and other (smooth) muscle, but it is the muscles of the musculoskeletal system that enable us to run, and when injured can cause us pain and poor function.

When a muscle is activated it produces movement. Each muscle helps create a particular movement, and produces different amounts of force, at different rates. The larger the (cross-sectional diameter of a) muscle, the more force it can produce.

Skeletal muscle can be classified into type 1 (slow twitch) and type 2 (fast twitch) muscle. Those with a greater percentage of type I fibers would theoretically be suited to long-distance running events, while someone born with a greater percentage of type 2 muscle fibers probably have an advantage during sprint events. Aerobic exercise uses oxygen to produce fuel for the muscles to move, and involves exercising at a level that does not require maximal output from the muscles. When we run flat out (sprint), or do any other anaerobic activity, the muscles are not capable of maintaining this for long periods of time.

When we run, although we use trunk, breathing and arm muscles, we are predominantly using muscles below the waist, and these are therefore asked to do the most work and are most susceptible to injury. Thus, most muscle injuries in runners are in the legs, with calf, hamstring and quadriceps the most common for various reasons.

Delayed onset muscle soreness (DOMS) is a pain or discomfort usually felt 24-72hrs after heavy or unaccustomed exercise. Most people would get some DOMS after their first marathon. I could hardly get down the stairs after mine, or in their quads if they did a lot of downhill running having not done any for a while, or might get DOMS in a few muscle groups if they played squash having not played for a while. DOMS is caused by tiny tears in the muscle fibres and settle by themselves after a few days. Sometimes ice baths, compression clothing, and chocolate milkshakes (or commercial recovery drinks) immediately after the provoking exercise are used to decrease the severity of DOMS.

Bruising in a muscle is known as a contusion. It is almost always caused by a direct blow onto a muscle. These are often called "dead legs" or "corked thigh" depending where in the world you are from. Pain, swelling, and bruising are often present. Ice, strapping, elevating the limb, and taking paracetamol/ acetoaminophen can help limit the severity of symptoms.

Sometimes forces can cause the structure of the muscle to be disrupted. This often occurs if the muscle is stretched suddenly. A muscular "strain" or tear can result. These are usually acute injuries, but chronic tears can occur.

Muscle tear symptoms include

- Sharp pain when an injury occurred (think of a footballer pulling a hamstring/ "hammie")
- Stiffness in the area
- Swelling and bruising
- Less movement in the area affected

There are different degrees of injury. Sometimes the muscle is merely stretched, while at other times some of the muscle fibers are torn, and occasionally all the fibers in a muscle will tear which is called "rupture" or "grade 3".

For the first 48 hours after injury, sensible measures would include PRICE

- **P**rotect from further injury
- **R**est and avoid exercise and excessive use of the muscle involved.
- **I**ce. Apply ice/ frozen peas to the sore area straight away and for 10 minutes twice a day. This will limit bleeding and further damage
- **C**ompression. This could be an elasticated bandage or similar
- **E**levation. The swelling can be taken away from the muscle by having the affected muscle above the level of your heart (for example put a pillow under your legs when sleeping).

Paracetamol/ acetoaminophen can be helpful as a painkiller, but non-steroidal anti-inflammatory drugs (NSAIDs) like ibuprofen should be avoided as they can encourage bleeding. Likewise, AVOID sitting in a hot bath. Notice the next time you are in a bath how the veins in your arm swell up. This is to help the body lose heat. If a muscle that is already bleeding is put in a hot bath, the damaged blood vessels are wider open and more bleeding and damage will occur. Likewise if you have DOMS then ice is better than a hot bath as this limits the damage.

If a muscle is still sore or you don't have the same range of movement after 48 hours, it is worth seeing a physio, your GP, or a sports medicine doctor to confirm the diagnosis, and give you specific exercises. Muscles do not show up well on x-ray. If the problem has been going on for some time, an ultrasound or MRI can help with the diagnosis. Once a diagnosis is made, correct exercises can help build up strength and function in the muscle again.

Ligaments

Ligament injuries are much less common in runners than tendon or muscle injuries. Ligaments connect bones to other bones, providing stability to a joint. They are made of similar tissue to tendons (connective tissue). Having more stretch in your ligaments (being "double-jointed") increases susceptibility to injury. The ligaments on the outside of your ankle are easily the most commonly damaged ones in runners- this can be while out running or often when playing other sport or dancing etc.

Ligaments are usually damaged as an acute (sudden) injury, for example when twisting your ankle. Other ligaments (like the cruciate ligaments inside the knee) are not commonly injured whilst running, but are often injured in contact sports, or sports in which sudden changes of direction are needed like such as hockey and football. Ligaments, like muscles, can be stretched, partly torn, or completely torn ("ruptured"). The ligament may not heal properly and leave a joint that is not stable, for example if you have twisted your ankle before, it is more likely to happen again as the ligament is not as strong.

Often it will be your physio or doctor who tells you that you have a ligament injury. You will report pain around a joint, and often a twisting injury to an ankle or knee. If you are not able to walk without a heavy limp you will probably need an x-ray to make sure no bones are broken.

Treatment of ankle and other ligament injuries depends on which ligament is affected, and how badly it has been torn, but often the PRICE approach is tried until a doctor or physio can be seen. If you cannot walk on it, or you are sore over the bony bits then you probably need to go to the Emergency Department for an X-ray.

PRICE (ligaments)

- **P**rotect from further injury- get the bus home if you twist your ankle badly!
- **R**est. Avoid exercise until the swelling has settled.

- **I**ce. Apply ice/ frozen peas to the sore area straight away and for 10 minutes twice a day. This will limit bleeding and further damage.
- **C**ompression. This could be an elasticated bandage or similar
- E- Elevation. The swelling can be taken away by having the affected area above the level of your heart (for example put a pillow under your legs when sleeping).

If you have a ligament injury it is important to take advice from a physio regarding exercises you can do to strengthen the ligament and the joint affected. This makes it much less likely to recur. It is also advised to wear an ankle brace for 6 months, and do rehab exercises for any bad ankle sprain. Occasionally if a ligament has completely ruptured, surgery may be considered.

Bursa

Bursae (singular= bursa) are small fluid-filled pockets that function to decrease friction between bones and tendons, or other structures. They allow tissues to glide over each other. There are many around each joint in the human body and, like any other tissue, they can become injured.

In runners the bursae are usually injured due to overuse/ biomechanical overload. Common sites of bursa injury include the front of the hip, bursitis causing symptoms at the iliotibial band on the outside of the knee, and a swollen bursa causing symptoms at the front of the knee (infrapatella) and where the achilles tendon joins the heel bone (retrocalcaneal bursitis).

Typical symptoms include pain and or swelling in the area, usually after an increase in the amount of exercise, a change in the intensity of exercise, or due to biomechanical factors. Once the cause is removed, symptoms often settle, although it can be difficult to tell if the pain is coming from a bursa, a nearby tendon, or another structure.

A simple strategy that can help includes PRICE

- **P**rotect from further injury.
- **R**elative rest. If the symptoms have been brought on by sudden increase in exercise, decrease this back to a level that did not bring symptoms on.
- **I**ce. Apply ice/ frozen peas to the sore area for 10 minutes twice a day.
- **C**ompression. This could be an elasticated bandage or similar.
- **E**levation. The swelling can be taken away from the area by having the affected area above the level of your heart (for example put a pillow under your legs when sleeping).

Where available, an ultrasound can help clarify the diagnosis. If the pain fails to settle with simple measures such as the above, together with physio input then a steroid injection can often help.

Cartilage

The skeleton of a shark is composed of cartilage rather than bone although sharks are not much good at running. In humans cartilage is found in many places, but importantly it is found in joints where it can function as a shock absorber to decrease forces on other structures. It is also found in the rib cages, and in the (intervertebral) discs of the back. It is less hard and more flexible than bone but compared to muscle it is less flexible and has a poorer blood supply.

Injuries can occur to the cartilage that lines a joint (articular cartilage) or the specialist sports cartilage that exists in certain places for example the menisci of the knee. Both the articular cartilage and the sports-type cartilage can be damaged by a sudden force causing a sudden injury or can be more gradually worn down in an overuse type injury. Cartilage has a poor blood supply, so it does not heal very well.

In an acute/ sudden injury, if cartilage has been damaged it is usually very sore, but requires medical input to clarify what structure has been damaged. Sometimes a damaged part of sports cartilage may be removed or repaired by an operation.

In a chronic wear and tear type problem to cartilage, the affected joint (usually the knee, ankle or hip) in runners may become sore and swollen, and the amount it can be moved might be restricted. If it completely wears out, bone can rub against bone. Osteoarthritis (wear and tear arthritis) can result from cartilage damage in a joint.

People often say that doing too much running causes wear and tear arthritis, but in fact this is rarely true. It is true that if you already have cartilage damage from a previous injury, or you are running 140km a week or more then the risk can be increased, but conversely wear and tear arthritis is actually much more common in those that are overweight or obese, and doing a bit of running actually prevents joints "rusting up" rather than necessarily causing "wear and tear". If you have been told you have a cartilage problem it is worth seeing a doctor, as advice is dependent on the type of the injury and it is very difficult to diagnose yourself.

4) Specific injuries

Achilles tendinopathy

Achilles tendinopathy is a common overuse injury often felt over the achilles tendon itself. This tendon stretches from your calf to your heel bone. It is one of, if not the most common injury in runners. "Tendinopathy" is when the tendon is grumbling rather than when it has snapped or torn.

Achilles tendinopathy presents with gradual onset of activity-related pain over the tendon that can often be "run through" but worsens with prolonged and continued training. The area is sore when pressed on or pinched, and may feel stiff particularly in the mornings which may improve with movement. There may be swelling at the point it attaches to the heel ("insertional"), or 2-6 cm further up ("mid-portion").

The table below shows some things that make it more likely that Achilles tendinopathy will occur, some clues to the diagnosis, and potential treatments

Presdisposing factors	Symptoms	Potential treatments
Increasing mileageIncreasing intensityHilly based trainingUneven groundPrevious Achilles problemsHyperpronation and other biomechanical errorsChange in running shoeChange in running styleObesity	Pain/ tender only over the AchillesStiff in morningsSore at start of run then can "run through it" then stiffens upSore when pinchedSwollenCan be hot	Address predisposing factorsDecrease mileage and add cross-training on bike, or cross-trainer, or swimPOLICEProtect from further injury OptimalLoad (see below)IceClever stuff- see belowElevation of leg when sleeping and restingOptimal load consists of exercises given to you by your physio. These are often "eccentric/ Alfredson Heel drop exercises" or Heavy Slow ResistanceClever stuff can include medications like ibuprofen tablets or gel, doxycycline, or Glyceryl Trinitrate patches. Strapping can often help.Certain injections can help if the above don't and very occasionally surgery is contemplated.

If you think you are getting Achilles tendinopathy, try and eliminate any of the predisposing factors you have, and try the basic treatments. It can often help to see a sports medicine doctor or physio to confirm the diagnosis (sports doctors will often confirm the diagnosis with a portable ultrasound machine), and guide your treatment, while helping eliminate predisposing factors. A biomechanical assessment will usually be part of the assessment.

Front of knee pain

Most runners will have episodes of pain at the front of their knee at some point. Along with achilles tendinopathy it is the complaint I see most at my clinic. Most of these issues are due to either patellofemoral pain syndrome, or patella tendinopathy. We will discuss these in turn, and briefly mention rarer causes.

Patellar tendinopathy

Patellar tendinopathy is damage to the tendon that joins the kneecap (patella) to the shin bone (tibia). It is common (and underestimated as a cause) in runners, and is very common in sports such as basketball and netball. It is due to repetitive forces on the tendon causing very small tears, or other damage and swelling.

Causes

Patellar tendinopathy is a common overuse injury. Jumping causes repeated strain to the patellar tendon resulting in changes to its structure such as small tears or cysts.

You're more likely to get patellar tendinopathy if you have:

- Recently changed your training programme.
- Shortened the length of your rest times.
- Problems with body movement (biomechanics).
- Poor muscle flexibility

Treatment

Patellar tendinopathy doesn't usually get better on its own, so it's important to seek medical treatment. A sports medicine professional, such as a physio or sports medicine doctor, will be able to diagnose the problem and give you a treatment plan. This will involve an exercise programme, usually strengthening exercises, and massage.

A biomechanical assessment may be recommended, as well as treatment from a podiatrist to prevent the injury from happening again. A podiatrist is a healthcare professional who specialises in treating lower leg, ankle and foot conditions.

There's no quick fix for patellar tendinopathy. You may need a period of rehabilitation before your symptoms go completely. However, the earlier you get treatment, the quicker your recovery is likely to be.

Do

- Use ice on the area just below your kneecap until the swelling goes down. Don't apply ice directly to your skin as it can give you an 'ice burn' Place a cloth between the ice and skin.

- Stretch your thighs and calf muscles regularly.

Don't

- Ignore the problem. The pain often gets better as the tendon warms up when you exercise. However, this may cause further damage, leading to more pain and a longer recovery time.
- Continue with high impact exercises that aggravate your knee, for example running and jumping.

Predisposing factors	Symptoms	Potential treatments
Increasing mileage

Increasing intensity

Other change in training program

Jumping sports (i.e.volleyball, basketball) or heavy "squats" in gym

Previous similar problems

Biomechanical errors

Change in running shoe

Change in running style

Obesity | Pain worst just below kneecap

Worse with jumping/ squatting

Stiff/ tightness around knee

Worse at start of exercise, then improves

Sore after longer bouts of exercise

Worse on downhills | Address predisposing factors

Decrease running mileage, and maintain aerobic fitness on bike/ cross trainer/ swim

POLICE
Protect from further injury by decreasing mileage
Optimal
Load (see below)
Ice
Clever stuff- see below
Elevation of leg when sleeping and resting

Optimal load consists of exercises given to you by your physio. These are often "eccentric" or Heavy Slow Resistance

Clever stuff can include medications like ibuprofen tablets or gel, doxycycline, or GTN patches. Strapping can often help.

Certain injections can help if the above don't and very occasionally surgery is contemplated. |

If you think you are getting patellar tendinopathy, try and eliminate any of the predisposing factors you have, and try the basic treatments. It can often help to see a sports medicine doctor or physio to confirm the diagnosis (sports doctors will often confirm the diagnosis with a portable ultrasound machine), and guide your treatment, while helping eliminate predisposing factors.

Patellofemoral pain syndrome

Patellofemoral pain syndrome is so common it is often known as runner's knee "runner's knee". It causes pain at the front of the knee. It is a term used to describe a variety of causes, including bony problems, poor alignment, and muscular and cartilage issues.

You may notice a theme, with most of these overuse problems. Many of the same factors predispose to injury, and the potential treatments are similar.

Presdisposing factors	Symptoms	Potential treatments
Downhill running	Pain worst at front of knee- often both sides	Address predisposing factors
Increasing mileage	Worse with squatting	Protect from further injury
Increasing intensity	Stiff/ tightness around knee	Decrease mileage to previously tolerated level
Other change in training program	Worse with continued running (doesn't "ease off")	Consider using cross trainer or bike to maintain aerobic fitness
Previous similar problems	Sore after longer bouts of exercise	Rehab exercises given by physio which often include quads and gluteal strengthening
Biomechanical errors- muscular imbalances, wide "q angle of knee", hyper-pronation	Worse on downhills	Ice after each run
Change in running shoe		If your symptoms have been present for some time, your doctor may order an x-ray to exclude wear and tear arthritis
Change in running style		
Obesity		Strapping
		Surgery only a last resort

Iliotibial band syndrome

Iliotibial band syndrome (ITBS) accounts for most pain on the outside of the knee in runners. It is an overuse injury. Repetitive movements cause compression and friction of the structures of the outside of the knee causing pain

Predisposing factors	Symptoms	Potential treatments
Downhill running	Pain at the outside of knee during running	Address predisposing factors
Increasing mileage		Decrease mileage to previously tolerated level or less
Running on a camber (one side of the road or a slope)	Often occurs at a reproducible distance	
	Sore to press on	Consider using cross trainer or bike/ swim to maintain aerobic fitness
Other change in training program	Worse with continued running (doesn't "ease off")	
Previous ITBS	Swelling may be present	Rehab exercises given by physio- often quads and gluteal strengthening
Biomechanical errors- muscular imbalances, overstriding		Ice after each run
Change in running shoe		If slow to get better consider corticosteroid injection with doctor
Change in running style		Surgery as last resort
Obesity		

Stress fractures

Stress fractures are not uncommon amongst runners and are usually overuse injuries in previously healthy bone. The most common sites for stress fracture are the shin bone (tibia), bones in the foot (in particular the metatarsals) although any bone below the waist can be affected. A less severe version is a "stress reaction", which is when tiny cracks in the bone occur without the surface of the bone being breached.

The bottom line is that unlike most other overuse injuries, you MUST stop running and consider cross-training to maintain fitness as otherwise stress fractures do not heal.

Presdisposing factors	Symptoms	Potential treatments
Increasing mileage, and/ or very high mileage	Sore to press on one particular point- often initially comes on gradually over days/ weeks	You need an accurate diagnosis. An x–ray may or may not show the problem
Increased intensity	Often occurs straight away on running and gets worse with continuing	An MRI is much more accurate
Previous stress fracture, stress reaction		If a stress fracture is confirmed you need to stop running until it has healed. This is the bottom line.
Female sex	Swelling may be present	
Low bone density		Consider using cross trainer or bike/ swim to maintain aerobic fitness
Hard surface		
Biomechanical errors- muscular imbalances, over-supination, unequal leg length		Address predisposing causes with your physio or doctor to lessen chances of another stress fracture in future
Change in running shoe		Occasionally surgery is required
Change in running style		
Obesity		

Shin splints

Shin splints is not actually a diagnosis, but is soreness commonly over the bone on the inside part of the lower leg. It can have several causes, and if you have pain over the bone in this area it is worth seeing a physio or sports medicine doctor to make sure there is not a stress fracture (break in the bone due to overuse).

There are 4 common causes of sore shins in runners. A sports doctor or physio can check that the pain is not due to a 1) a stress fracture, 2) overuse of the lower leg muscles (usually tibialis anterior) or 3) compression of blood vessels during exercise (compartment syndrome).

The majority of shin splints are caused by irritation of the lining of the bone (periosteum) and nearby structures. It has been given a variety of medical and profane names, most commonly medial tibial stress syndrome (MTSS).

Medial Tibial Stress Syndrome

Presdisposing factors	Symptoms	Potential treatments
New to regular running or marching

Increasing mileage

Increased intensity

Previous "shin splints"

Female gender

Low bone density

Hard or hilly surface

Biomechanical errors- muscular imbalances, hyper-pronation, unequal leg length

Change in/ unsuitable running shoe

Change in running style

Obesity | Sore to press over the shin bone (tibia), but over a larger area than a fingertip. (being sore over just one place makes a stress fracture more likely)

Often occurs straight away on running and gets worse with continuing

Swelling may be present but only a small amount | Alter and improve any predisposing factors

Decrease running distance and intensity to a level that pain is minimal

Consider cross training/ cycling/ swimming to maintain fitness

Ice, and painkillers

If you are worried it could be a stress fracture see a doctor or physio. They may arrange an X-ray or MRI if they are not sure themselves

A coach, physio or doctor can work to reduce predisposing causes

Surgery should not be required. Modifying what you do will usually bring results. |

Blisters

Blisters are due to friction and have affected almost every runner at some time during their running careers. Over 40% of runners doing a marathon will get a blister. They can lead to pain, infection and perhaps most painfully a 'did not finish'. If you can avoid as many predisposing factors as possible, then these problems are less likely.

Presdisposing factors	Symptoms	Potential treatments
New to regular running or marching

Racing at a faster pace than you are used to | Pain over affected area

Fluid collecting under skin | Alter and improve any predisposing factors

Do some training at 'race pace'.

Wear in shoes prior to long |

New/ unsuitable shoes		runs/ races
Increasing mileage		Increase mileage slowly
Previous blisters		Get a comfy pair of shoes and (wicking) socks
Sweaty feet		
Hard, sandy or hilly surface		Antiperspirant (deodorant)
		Train in conditions you will race in
Biomechanical errors- muscular imbalances,		Once a blister develops, I suggest cleaning the skin, and popping the blister with a sterile needle/ safety pin and let/ squeeze the fluid out. Keep the area clean and tape over it if you need to continue to race.
Carrying heavy rucksack		
Obesity		
		Some people use zinc oxide tape, others compede-type plasters.
		If the blister has pus coming out, or is very red, antibiotic cream or tablets is advised.

Chafing

Chafing is inflammation of the skin due to friction when skin surfaces rub together. We have all seen the pictures of the man with the white shirt and red marks from his nipples rubbing the skin. Chafing often occurs in the groin, nipple and underarm areas, and the back if wearing a backpack.

The good news is that it can be largely prevented by drying likely affected areas before running, applying petroleum jelly (vaseline or similar) to groin and under arm areas, and wearing a suitable bra (women) and tape (men) in the nipple area.

If chafing has developed, keep the area clean to prevent infection, and a mild hydrocortisone cream can help. Tape or Vaseline any areas if you need to run while areas are still troublesome.

Part 3- Nutrition and Hydration

1) Introduction

Sound diet and good nutritional strategies are essential to help you perform at your best. Diet affects performance and the foods you choose during training and racing will affect how well you train and compete. Getting the right amount of energy and protein to support and promote muscle tissue adaptations to training, as well as to stay healthy and perform to your best level is important. Runners' nutritional needs are individual, and will change depending on the amount of training you are doing, what your work involves etc.

In general a varied and wholesome nutrient-rich diet that meets your energy needs and is based largely on vegetables, fruits, beans, legumes, grains, lean animal meats, oils and carbohydrate should ensure an adequate intake of all essential vitamins and minerals. Runners who eat an adequate balanced diet usually have no need for supplementation.

This diagram shows how to utilise various food groups, and when.

GOOD RUNNING NUTRITION

CORE
EAT AS MUCH OF THESE FOODS AS YOU WANT AND AS OFTEN AS YOU LIKE
All vegetables that grow above the ground, fresh fruit and berries

FLUIDS
VITAL FOR EXERCISE PERFORMANCE AND RECOVERY- DRINK WHEN YOU ARE THIRSTY
Water, rehydration drinks (ONLY when training), tea especially green tea, no added sugar diluting juice, diluted fruit juice.

FUEL
SUPPLIES THE ENERGY FOR TRAINING, USE DURING EXERCISE OVER AN HOUR DURATION, OR AFTER PROLONGED EXERCISE

Pasta	Bulgar wheat
Root vegetables	Porridge/oats
Rice	Jams & honey
Cereals	Fresh & dried fruit
Breads	Fruit juice
Noodles	Sports drinks (diluted)
Quinoa	Cereal bars
Cous cous	Energy gels

RECOVER
SUPPLIES NUTRIENTS FOR GROWTH AND RECOVERY- ESPECIALLY AFTER A LONG RUN OR HARD SESSION

Milk	Chicken/poultry
Eggs	Beef
Yogurts	Fish
Skimmed milk powder	Soy
Cottage cheese	
Beans & pulses	

RESTORE
HELPS MAINTAIN HEALTHY FUNCTION- EAT BUT NOT TOO MUCH

Salmon	Extra virgin olive oil	Spices and chillies	Cherry juice
Mackerel and sardines	Linseed oil	Avocado	Large oats
Grass-fed beef and poultry	Nuts and seeds	Beetroot	Bulgar wheat
			Quinoa

CORE- Fresh fruit, berries, and vegetables that grow above the ground contain essential nutrients and goodness and are unlikely to cause weight gain. Eat as many of this group as you like.

FLUIDS- Staying hydrated helps avoid illness and injury. Drink when you are thirsty. Most of the time water works well, while sports drinks (diluted), rehydration drinks, diluted fruit juice might help after or during long periods of exercise.

FUEL- Supplies energy when needed, but eating too much fuel in relation to energy expenditure may lead to weight gain. Use this food group when you have earned it expending energy, or are about to earn it.

RECOVER- After a long run or a hard session these protein-containing foods can help muscles repair themselves and the body recover.

RESTORE- These foods maintain healthy function, and are generally healthy. Some are calorie dense, so balance health with potential calorie intake.

General Advice

Top tips

- Plan your approach to your nutrition: consider what you are doing that week and each day, and what types of foods might be helpful. If you don't think you are getting this right, keep a diary.
- Let your partner/ flatmates know your general nutrition plan, so they can help or at least not accidentally sabotage.
- Try to stick by guidelines as often as possible. Choose places to stay and eat that are likely to help with this

- Have some fruit or vegetables (which are an excellent source of key vitamins and minerals) with every meal if possible. Even simple things like fruit on breakfast cereal help
- Make sure you have water available. This is generally preferable to sports drinks except during races or training runs of over an hour.
- If you are ill, it is twice as important to eat well

2) Hydration specifics

- During races, drink to thirst. There has been commercial interest in advising people to remain completely hydrated during competition, but more people have died of over-drinking (due to a condition called hyponatraemia) than dehydration. The body is extremely good at letting you know when you need more fluid. Have fluid available, but drink to thirst.
- Almost every elite marathon performance has been achieved with a degree of dehydration, as it is hard for the stomach to tolerate the amount of fluid sweated out when running quickly. Haile Gebrselaisse was at least 8% dehydrated when smashing the world marathon record in Berlin.
- During races having carbohydrate (ideally about 6% solution) in your drink is an easy way of getting additional fuel on board and is preferable to water.

3) Nutrition specifics

- Have a carbohydrate and protein-based drink, meal or snack soon (within 1 hr.) of completing a run of over 1 hr, or a race. This could include a milkshake, or a sandwich/ baked potato with tuna/ chicken etc.
- If doing a race over half-marathon distance carbo-load the night before. There is no benefit if the race is shorter.
- During a training run of half-marathon distance or longer, take small amounts of carbohydrate often to replace fuel stores.
- Find food that works for you these sorts of races, as even if the food is scientifically amazing, it is useless if you can't stomach it.
- Professional athletes usually have their iron and vitamin D levels checked regularly. Prioritise iron, and vitamin D rich foods.
- If you are vegetarian, have heavy periods, or are running more than 70 miles per week, get your iron checked at least yearly. Low iron stores increase risk of infection and poor endurance even if you are not 'anaemic' (low red blood count).

Here is a table describing how some food types may help optimise training, performance and recovery, with the usual caveat that individual athletes may benefit from slightly different advice based on many factors.

Do Use

Substance	When Indicated	How to Take
Carbohydrate	During, and after prolonged training or competition.	Carb based food (banana, cereal bar, sandwich etc) Sports drink with 5-8% carbs
Fluid with electrolyte	During prolonged training or competition in the heat	Water, with electrolyte sachet Sports drink
Carbohydrate and protein	Between 0 and 60 minutes after heavy session or run longer than an hour	3:1 Carb:protein ratio ideal. Chicken/ tuna/ egg sandwich, meat with potatoes

Use when indicated

Substance	When Indicated	How to Take
Lyprinol/ Lyprinol Sport	After over 20km runs to decrease inflammation and muscle soreness	As per packaging
Iron (ferrous)	Ferritin level low <40ng/ ml	Depending on level. Consult doctor.
Multivitamin	Very poor diet	Single multivitamin including iron, zinc, magnesium.
Zinc	Onset of common cold/ flu	2 zinc lozenges/ day.
Vitamin D	Low Vit D level <75nmol/l	Prescribed tablets
Probiotic	When unwell, diarrhoea, or taking antibiotics	Yakulk/ actimel

Don't Bother- Ginseng, chromium, specific amino acids, carnitine, almost everything else. See next section on Prevention.

- Be <u>very</u> careful with supplements if you are doing a race where there is drug testing. None of the substances listed is banned, but unless they have been fully tested then contaminated supplements do occur and have cost Olympic medals.

Part 4- Travel and First Aid considerations

1) Introduction

A much-neglected aspect of preparation for a race (especially one that is abroad) is travel. A long journey by car, or travelling to an event abroad can have significant health and performance implications. Simple strategies applied well will decrease the chance of illness, fatigue and jet lag. Some time spent planning the travel considerations of each event will help you perform your best. The tables below can be used as a checklist.

2) Before setting off

Check	Tick when done
Check you have enough of your own medications	
If you are a professional athlete check you have valid therapeutic use exemption T.U.E if needed. Check no further vaccinations are needed.	
Pack suggested Travel Kit (including anti-histamines, painkillers etc)	
Pack essential items and medications in carry-on luggage	
Pack necessary and trusted snacks/ gels, if needed	
Plan flights/ travel to allow acclimatisation and rest prior to event	
Avoid excess alcohol on flights, and move legs regularly	
Use "First Defence" on flights (1 puff each nostril before flight and every 6 hours).	

3) Suggested medical travel kit

This simple medical travel kit contains a few basics that will help prevent and treat illness. Have it in the house, and take it with you in your hand luggage when you travel.

Item	When	How many
Hand Sanitiser gel	Flights, meals, post toilet	1 bottle
First Defence spray	Pre- flight	1
(Plain) Vitamin C, 1 gram	Head cold, one tab per day	16 tablets
Paracetamol 500mg	Pain, fever, two, 4x per day	16 tablets
Ibuprofen 400mg	Pain, fever, inflammation. One, 3x per day (not on race day)	16 tabs
Antacid	Indigestion	10
Cetirizine 10mg	Itch, hay fever, allergy. One daily.	10
Loperamide	Diarrhoea, 2mg, one after each loose poo	10
Lip salve	Chapped lips	1
Sun cream	As needed	1
Compression clothes	During flights >3hrs	Skins or similar
Eye Mask	Sleeping aid	1
Ear Plugs	Sleeping aid	2 pairs
Foam Roller	Treat injury	1

Source: **Dr Andrew Murray**

4) Once you arrive to train or race abroad

- Adjust body clock to local time
- Ensure access to healthy and adequate food and bottled water

5) *Jet lag and sleep*

International travel has a big impact on our body clocks. Jet lag increases the chance of picking up an infection, increases muscle fatigue and can stop us performing our best. This can be reduced significantly with simple suggested measures.

- Plan schedule considering possible impact of Jet Lag
  - allow adequate time on arrival to adjust
  - plan only light exercise/ practice on day of arrival if long flight and jet lag likely
- Plan travel with direct flights if possible/ or with minimal delays
- Consider gradually adjusting to destination time in days before long flight
- Use ear plugs and eye mask on flights, especially overnight flights
- Avoid excess alcohol and caffeine on flight
- Switch to destination time on arrival for sleep, meals and training

Part 5- The Mind Game

1) *You versus yourself*

Every runner has a different aim. Some look purely' for enjoyment and relaxation; others wish to improve their health, while the competitive instinct is a powerful motivator whether the aim is a personal best or an Olympic medal.

Most runners focus on physical preparation, but being prepared mentally is time well invested in being the best you can be. Following the example of many elite stars, runners are looking at how they can prepare mentally, and a few key themes have emerged

The first thing is to recognise that while talent and genetic ability play a part, most of any success – be that achieved in anything from completing your first 5km, to winning – is in your hands. A great example is Steven Way, who went from being, by his own admission, a 17 stone couch surfer to a leading international athlete in his thirties. It is about putting the effort in to achieve improvement, and doing the right things consistently. This does not guarantee success, but it makes it much more likely. You can be your own best friend, or your own worst enemy.

2) *Clear focus*

Knowing what you want to achieve makes this outcome more likely. If you do not know where you want to go, arriving at this ideal destination will not happen. Do not leave this to chance, and think about what you want to achieve in the short and long term.

Once you know where the destination is, you can work out how to get there. This focus is a powerful motivating force. Floyd Woodrow, in his excellent book "*Elite*" (2012) discusses the logic of having a clear focus, and then working out the key components of getting there, recognising spelling out what the desired destination is can motivate and help you work out the key steps.

If you were starting in London, and wished to drive to Paris, this might involve filling your car with fuel, buying a ferry ticket, and buying a route map (or putting the address into sat nav). Likewise, if your plan is to finish your first marathon then the key steps might be to map out a training plan (and stick to it), and eat small amounts of carbohydrates often during the race itself.

A clear focus guides specificity in how you train. Mo Farah is an excellent example of an athlete with a clear focus. Although his 5000 and 10000metres times are only the 31st, and 16th fastest of all time, he has 2 Olympic and 3 World titles. In his book he talks openly about the specificity of his training- and that his clear focus is on championship races. With these types of races typically being slower and demanding a faster finish, Farah has worked relentlessly to develop a killer last lap.

This can work for us too. If our focus is on a long race, some long training runs will be in order. If it is a mountain race, then training on similar terrain is beneficial. Knowing exactly what you want to achieve helps us think through, and do the things that will help us achieve them.

3) *Break it down*

Once you have a clear focus on achieving something for example finishing that first marathon, most find it helpful to break down the task into chunks.

That first finisher's medal (and the sore legs that go with it) are a memory few of us will forget. The mental image of crossing the line can be a powerful motivating factor during the race and in training, but 26.2miles or whatever you are training is a daunting prospect on the start line.

Breaking a task of this size down into chunks has been shown to increase the chances of you getting there. The human brain loves ticking off little successes along the way, so concentrating on getting the first week of training done, then the second, and so on stops the brain thinking of the longer and harder runs that need to be done closer to race time.

This works during a race/ event also. I remember standing on the start line before running 2659 miles from the north of Scotland to the Sahara and thinking the task was impossible. Over 34 miles every day for almost 80 days. What worked was literally to break the challenge into chunks, and give myself a small reward with each marker achieved. Each 10km, I earned something nice to eat, and mentally ticked off another box in my head. When the weather was disgusting or injuries were playing up, I could think of the 3 or 4 small wins I had gained that day, rather than fret about the 2000 miles to go.

I also remember my first half-marathon, and the advice given to me by a fellow runner, Suzie, who I met on the course. Seeing I was struggling after about 10km, she said "just keep ticking off each kilometre, each lamp post. it's easier that way." Mentally seeing that next goal coming into view was much more pleasant than thinking with dread that I was less than half way. Each step is one step closer to the finish line, and that goes for training as well as racing.

Break the challenge down.

4) Logic and emotion

"*The Chimp Paradox*" (2012) by the renowned sports psychiatrist Steve Peters offers a system to understand why we behave the way we do, and if we understand the way our brain works, then this insight allows us to control unhelpful thoughts and be more productive in what we are doing; be that making rockets, performing operations, or running races.

Peters (who is often credited by a variety of individuals and organisations such as Sir Chris Hoy, Ronnie O'Sullivan and Liverpool FC) talks of our emotional and irrational side as being our "chimp" which is stronger than logical and rational side which Peters labels as the human. Both the chimp and the human can be helpful at different times. Using emotion positively is a part of the success that host nations invariably achieve during a home Olympic Games, but the chimp can also hijack progress with emotional thinking.

Too many times to count have I decided not to go and train because it's been raining, or given in to the chimp urging me to walk when I have been tired during a race. Being aware of when you are being hijacked by your emotional side, and deliberately thinking as logically as possible at these times is a lesson I've taken from Peters. I'll talk to myself "why should I walk? logically is my foot actually that sore? I've run with worse, if I eat a little food that should help avoid hitting the wall, I've run in worse weather conditions, just keep going, you'll thank yourself for it later".

Paradoxically, incredible feats have been achieved partly by harnessing the power of your emotional side. Stories abound of ladies lifting up cars to protect their child, or individuals or teams performing amazing things to remember a friend or relative. Channelling emotional energy can motivate and inspire us, a tactic much used by football and running coaches. The trick is to recognise the way your mind is working, and use this to your advantage.

5) The growth mentality

Talent alone does not bring success. At the highest level, it is necessary, but not sufficient. American psychologist Carol Dweck has described "the growth mindset" as a critical determinant of doing well in many aspects of life. The key idea is that great results can be delivered through hard work and an active effort to develop yourself and improve. Those with this "growth mindset" view setbacks as a learning experience, and are resilient. The opposite is the "fixed mindset" in which people believe that they are born with ability or not, and are less likely to apply efforts to improve.

A growth mindset can be learned. This is excellent news for us runners, because by learning to adopt and develop a growth mindset, we are likely to view ourselves more positively and will be more successful. We will also view events that did not go perfectly as a learning experience, and carry on trying rather than putting it down to a lack of ability. Believing that practicing and learning can lead to improvement in your running will get results. Imperfections are not shameful. Do not see what you can do now as the limit of your ability. A motto adopted by Kenyan runners is "train hard, win easy". Very few, if any, outstanding athletes will claim that talent is the number 1 reason for their success. Many more, including 5 x world champion John Ngugi will claim that hard work is the cornerstone, while looking at others and working out how to improve is a key driver of improvement.

Hard work is necessary, but not sufficient to be successful. Smart work is also required. I know lots of runners who trained very hard, but not very smartly. This relates to specificity. The training has to be directly related to the goal you are trying to achieve. Doing 100 miles a week all at 7min/mile pace is hard work, but if you want to run a marathon at 6min/mile pace that sort of training isn't too smart.

Part 6 – What Makes Champions

1) Introduction - lessons from East Africa

Although modest in geographical terms, Kenya is a giant in the world of middle and long-distance running. At the 2011 Athletics World Championships, Kenya won 17 medals, with no less fewer than 11 of them going to athletes based in the tiny village of Iten. It is a statistic that borders on the absurd. Medallists, from one World Championship, from one village with 4000 residents. In the same year, all 20 of the fastest marathon times, and 66 of the 100 fastest times were run by Kenyans from the Rift Valley. This is an utterly outrageous statistic. Imagine if all of the world's top 20 footballers, and 66 of the top 100 were British players from Wales. More recently, at the 2013 Athletics World Championships, Kenya won more medals than Great Britain, China and Spain combined. This is not a temporary phenomenon: Kenyan athletes have dominated distance running since the 1970's. Of the best ever 20 times set in each of 1500 metres, 3000 metre steeplechase, 5000 metres, 10000 metres, half-marathon and marathon, over 50 per cent have been recorded by Kenyans.

The Rift Valley of Kenya remains the greatest, most concentrated, production line of talent in world sport. Elite performance does not happen by chance, and the reasons for this outrageous success are becoming more clearly understood. Having grown up in Kenya, I've subsequently spent time working as a sports medicine doctor with international teams on high altitude training camps, as well as learning from and spending time with some of the best athletes on earth, and coaches like Colm O'Connell who has guided more than 30 athletes to World Championship glory. This chapter explores the defining reasons behind the East African success, while also looking at elite performance in other runners such as Great Britain's Mo Farah, and lessons from other elite individuals and teams in sport. Whilst you may or may not harbour aspirations to be a World or Olympic champion, the reasons the elite get to where they are interesting, and hold clues to how people of any ability can perform to their best.

Iten stadium

Picture Toby Smith

Many theories have emerged trying to explain the East African, and in particular Kenyan domination of middle and long distance events. Genetic factors, role modelling, residence at high altitude, the simple nutrition favoured locally, a relative lack of vehicular transport have all been cited, whilst others have even speculated that the Kalenjin tribe's history of cattle rustling can explain their success.

British athletes such as Mo Farah and Paula Radcliffe have tasted success at the highest level, but despite these successes, whilst East African runners have achieved faster times in greater numbers, fewer British and indeed North American runners are doing so. In 1984, 75 British runners achieved a sub 2hrs 20 minutes marathon, whilst in 2011 this figure stood at 10.

2) Why are the East Africans so fast?

Genetics?

It is often claimed that unique genetic characteristics are responsible for the consistent success of East African middle and long distance runners. Within Kenya, many ethnic groups exist, and success is most marked amongst a few tribes, notably the Kalenjin tribe. This is seen as proof that genetic factors are the major determinant of athletic success. Despite extensive investigation by research teams including Prof Yannis Pitsalidis and his team, superior genetic characteristics amongst East African runners have not been found, and are unlikely to be a major factor. Domination of middle distance (UK athletes in the 1980's) and long distance (Finnish athletes in the early 20th century) by different populations proves you do not need to be East African to be successful, but that a given population can dominate events for periods of time when environmental and cultural factors in that group are more favourable than anywhere else. So there is hope, just because Ethiopian and

Kenyan athletes are ruling the roost in these events at present, does not mean it will always be so!

Training Programs

Elite athletes worldwide, and in Kenya consistently say that there is no substitute for discipline and hard work, prioritising training as the major focus of their life. Almost every elite and sub-elite athlete I spoke with mentioned discipline, and some variation of a prevailing Kenyan motto "train hard, win easy." Edna Kiplagat who has won the last 2 female World Championship marathons, and five time World Champion John Ngugi both stated sticking closely to a proven training regime to be the single most important factor in their success. Many athletes in Iten train 2 or 3 times per day, which often includes a track session on Tuesdays, a fast session on Thursday, and a long run on Saturday. Sunday is often a rest day. Recovery and low-intensity running is at a very slow pace, with a wide difference between low and high-intensity sessions. Many a rank amateur like myself has run past Olympic 800m Champion David Rudisha during his slow runs, but his high-intensity work is blistering. Leading western coach and former elite runner Alberto Salazar feels that the volume of high-quality grassroots runners in Kenya permits coaches to suggest large training loads to athletes. Those that can tolerate them may gain adaption and improvement, whilst injuries to athletes take place in a deeper pool of talent. Simply put, if one athlete is injured there will likely be another to take their place. Emphasis is placed on rest, recovery, and adequate sleep which is widely considered part of training/ the job.

Whatever the training regime is that has been decided, it will be done. I've virtually never seen the top guys return early from a training run, turn the alarm clock back off and go back to sleep, or make any other excuse no matter how valid it might be.

Coaching

Most athletes who reside in Iten are not from there originally, but were either enrolled as youngsters to a local school, or have subsequently arrived due to the altitude, training groups, and the culture of running in the village. Athletic talent and other key ingredients for success exist across the Rift Valley, but Iten has prospered due to structured talent identification, and grassroots programmes that bring talented youngsters to schools such as St Patrick's, a program honed by Brother Colm O'Connell, who has moulded the careers of over 30 World Champions. Brother Colm arrived in Kenya in 1976 as a missionary aiming to teach geography. He had no background in coaching or athletics but was seen as an excellent organiser and took over some of the coaching at a time when Kenya had not enjoyed any consistent success on the world stage. The school he worked at, St Patrick's School, became a production line of talent and started planting a tree for each World champion associated with the school. This now resembles a forest, given the number of world and Olympic champions who have graduated from St Patrick's.

Brother Colm is a modest and unassuming man, reluctant to take any credit for what has been achieved, but it is clear that the structures and guidance he has provided have not only promoted male and female athletics, but been life-changing for many individuals and communities in the region. His philosophy is to use athletics to create good people, whether they are talented and likely to succeed at a high level or not, instilling a love of sport and self-discipline. It is this philosophy articulated beautifully by Scotland's Chief Medical Officer Harry Burns who talked of a need to work with communities to unleash talent and community pride that helps create a large number of motivated grass roots talent in East Africa. It is easier to create strong children than mend broken men.

Coaching at elite level involves fewer experts than in the west, with noticeably less analysis and data crunching, and a sharp focus on training, rest and recovery. Coaches such as O'Connell and Yobes Ondieki –a former World champion and World Record holder- emphasize that systems and processes are important, but athletes are individuals, and different things work well for different people.

Rest and Recovery

Leading athletes jokingly claim to be World champions at sleeping, as well as at running. Some nap briefly after each session, and most ensure at least 8 hrs sleep every night. Multiple world record holder Lornah Kiplagat often sleeps for over 10hrs.

Observers note that top-class Kenyan athletes do little other than run, eat, and sleep. Leading author Toby Tanser, and legendary coach Colm O'Connell stress the importance of relaxation, and turning off. O'Connell actively encourages "doing nothing, relaxing physically and mentally" amongst his athletes, while Tanser feels a lack of distraction is important. Few Kenyan athletes study, or work in addition to running, and athletes very often live in Spartan training camps away from their family to ensure distraction is minimised. I often find myself getting less sleep than I need for one reason or another. Experts have shown that a number of things suffer greatly as a result of this, including ability to do difficult tasks, ability to concentrate and resistance to illness and injury. Whilst the world we live in is a busy place, getting the right amount of rest in recovery helps performance in work, is generally good for health and well-being, and is a cornerstone of running performance.

Diet and Body Shape (Anthropometrics)

The rural Kenyan diet as well as the typical Ethiopian diet has been studied extensively by Barry Fudge (Head of Endurance at UK Athletics) and others. Food consumed tends to be simple, fresh and locally sourced. Fresh fruit and vegetables are prominent, although many a childhood broken arm has occurred falling out of a mango tree trying to reach the fruit. Studies by Pitsalidis *et al]* in Kenyan and Ethiopian runners show a high carbohydrate content, and that runners meet most recommendations for endurance athletes for food and nutrient intake without any need to supplement. Over-eating, and taking in processed food is not common amongst the general public in rural East Africa, in contrast to Western Europe and North America. Wikipedia claims that there are 18450 McDonalds restaurants in the USA, 1250+ in the UK, and none in either Kenya or Ethiopia.

As a result of dietary factors and high levels of exercise, whilst 60% of Brits are overweight or obese, this figure is very low in Kenya. In fact, when studied in Nandi hills, the average Kenyan youngster had a low or normal bodyweight and a very high level of fitness which is not currently the case in Europe or North America. This leaves a large pool of potential athletes. Developing and elite athletes in Kenya predominantly eat the same simple diet as the population. They have therefore been exposed to this diet since a young age. Supplement use is less common.

Although East Africans do not typically have a larger capacity to process oxygen per minute (VO2 Max), they do typically run more economically, therefore requiring less oxygen to travel a given distance at a given speed. This advantage is largely due to diet, training, coaching and other factors, although the Kalenjins do typically have longer Achilles Tendons and small calf muscles which are biomechanically advantageous. David Epstein's excellent book "The Sports Gene, 2013" looks at this and other anthropometric considerations in other sports. There are some sports for example basketball that anthropometric considerations are of enormous importance. Epstein states that if you are over 7 foot tall, there is a 1 in 6 chance that you are playing NBA basketball right now emphasizing height as a characteristic that greatly improves your chance of high performance in this sport.

A lifetime of training

The vast majority of elite Kenyan athletes come from rural, peasant families. Many describe walking or running many miles to and from school every day, building up a lifetime of training. One in 200 Rift Valley citizens own a television, with studies of these populations showing that children from this area are highly physically active, and have low body mass index (BMIs) which is a measure of weight compared to height. Running is normal in Kenya in day to day life, in Iten it is rare for a child not to try and join in when a foreigner runs past. Even young children are incredibly fit. I remember a girl of 8 in school uniform and a pair of sandals running alongside me at 8 miles an hour. Many Kenyans run to get somewhere, whilst even in Iten, there are 800 professional athletes.

Altitude

People living at altitudes between 1500 and 2850 metres do have some advantage. Those who train at altitude effectively, perform better at altitude, and at sea level.

Altitudes between 1500 and 2850 metres are thought to allow a balance between helping to increase oxygen-carrying capacity and thus improving performance, whilst allowing training to be done at an intensity required to drive elite performance. Most Kenyan athletes are based in areas at such altitudes, at bases that include Iten, Eldoret, the Nandi hills region, and Kericho. The village of Bekoji, in Ethiopia, at 2810 metres has yielded household names such as Keninesa Bekele, Tirunesh Dibaba and many others. Non high-altitude natives (those not born at altitude, but who choose to live or train in these areas) also benefit. Mo Farah and Paula Radcliffe are documented to have spent considerable time at altitude, or in generated hypoxic environments for example, altitude tents. Time at specific altitudes, whether actual or in a generated environment, is beneficial and is widely used across most endurance sports including cycling, swimming and triathlon.

Prioritisation

Being a successful athlete is THE clear focus for successful athletes. Almost universally, those who have worked with champions identify their discipline and prioritisation of their athletic ambitions as key factors in their success. There are things that can help people run faster, but without hard work and dedication they are not sufficient. In Iten, almost all good-quality cars, and expensive houses are owned by athletes. Running is seen as one of the only ways to escape poverty, and be successful. Professional athletes will prioritise this as the most important thing in their lives, often living away from family and shunning other interests, whilst even amateur athletes will devote significant priority to their running. This is the norm in terms of athlete behaviour. As an amateur athlete, I trained, slept and ate better in Kenya. Back home I am more susceptible to distraction.

Role Modelling

Many of East Africa's foremost heroes are middle and long-distance runners. Whilst some children in Britain may wish to be the next Mo Farah, more wish to be the next David Beckham, or Kate Winslett. Legends like Haile Gebrselaisse, John Ngugi, David Rudisha and Edna Kiplagat offer heroes to aspire to, and hope that they too could be successful. One former double World Champion mentioned that he watched a friend win a Junior World Championship, and decided to start training as having run to school with his friend he knew he was faster.

Psychology. Aiming High

Perhaps due to the consistent success of their compatriots, Kenyan athletes aim high and then set about achieving it in an all or nothing approach. Highly ambitious targets are outlined by their top athletes, but this culture pervades amongst the sub-elites. Many athletes I spoke with believed they were potential world champions, even those whose results were modest at a local level. Often local races will set off at an outrageous pace with inevitable drop-outs often seeing failure in a positive light and becoming all the more determined. "I kept up with athlete X for 3 km; next time I will beat him". Setbacks are taken with a smile as a learning experience rather than failure- an example of a growth mentality.

3) *Lessons from other elite individuals*

Dave Brailesford

British Cycling in recent years has achieved unprecedented success both on the track, and in road racing. This has only been possible with outstanding and focussed leadership, and committed athletes that who aim high, involve the right people and are mentally and physically prepared to deliver under pressure.

Team principal Dave Brailesford is not afraid to aim high, committing publically to specific, measureable, and seemingly audacious goals. He challenged Team GB to be the most successful nation in cycling at the Beijing 2008 Olympics, then targeted a repeat of the most successful performance by a nation in London 2012. Additionally in 2010, he publically committed to a Team Sky rider winning the Tour de France by 2015. He lets all athletes and staff know what success would look like, and what team priorities are. Too many athletes do not know exactly what success would look like. This makes it more difficult to get there.

There appears to be no misunderstanding regarding priorities and focus. Expectations of athletes and staff are high but the support is there to back this up. This clarity of focus channels resources appropriately. A nation's ranking at Olympic Games are determined by gold medals not number of finalists. Thus, athletes focus squarely upon medals, and are disappointed when they do not achieve gold. Dave Brailesford does not aim for his athletes to reach finals, or finish second. He expects them to win, or help their team mates win.

Tough decisions are made to retain a focus on stated targets. Despite having leading sprinter Mark Cavendish in the team, the unswerving focus during the 2012 Tour de France was for team leader Sir Bradley Wiggins to win the tour- a decision that ultimately contributed to Cavendish leaving the team. During the London 2012 games, team GB's most successful cyclist of all time Sir Chris Hoy was left out of the individual sprint in favour of Jason Kenny. Important events, even world championships are deprioritised to retain a focus on the clear priorities for the team.

British/ Team Sky cycling involves the right people, and leaves no stone unturned. With the focus on improving performance, the "science of marginal gains" has been applied. Anything within the rules that can contribute to achieving stated goals is tested, and applied systematically if beneficial. Staff (and athletes) know clearly defined roles.

A growth mentality is part of the culture. The team has prioritised psychological training for athletes. Many cite the influence of psychiatrist Steve Peters in helping achieve a cohort of athletes who embrace challenge, are in control of their emotions, and deliver consistently under pressure. Challenge is viewed as an opportunity to learn, and adversity is planned for and problems solved. Chris Hoy's attributes include excellent peak power generation, acceleration, and an ability to sprint for relatively long periods, but his way of embracing setbacks with a calm resolve was equally important when his favoured "kilo" event was dropped from the Olympics, when he was left out of the London 2012 sprint event, or when Max Levy overtook him on the last lap of the keirin at London. Team mate Jason Quelly says "his perseverance, his dedication, his whole mindset – he just doesn't give in. That's what sets him apart."

Alberto Salazar

Alberto Salazar won 3 consecutive New York Marathons and a Boston Marathon in the 1980's, and currently coaches athletes such as Galen Rupp, and Mo Farah who regularly compete with, and defeat the cream of East African talent.

Salazar leaves no stone unturned in achieving optimum results. As an athlete he would try anything legal to gain an advantage, and is similarly rigorous in looking to improve his athletes. He acknowledges the volume of grass roots talent in East Africa, stating that Britain and the USA may have to polish their diamonds harder- directing focus towards key athletes, involving the right people, and taking advantage of technology to seize any advantage however marginal. Bringing a cryotherapy chamber to the London Olympics at considerable expense may have offered athletes like Rupp and Farah a competitive advantage in recovering from the 10000metres to compete successfully in the 5000metres. When the difference between gold and 4th can be less than 1%, every second counts.

(Salazar was one of the hardest runners I have known. He even came close to death on at least one occasion after running so hard).

Mo Farah

Mo Farah is tangible proof that lessons can be applied from top East African athletes, contributing to success on the highest stage. He has achieved a step change from gifted athlete to world number 1. There are myriad reasons for this, but prominent amongst them may be factors common to almost every great sportsman/woman.

Farah has benchmarked success on Olympic and World Championship gold. He has triumphed when it matters most. A knowledge of championship racing and working specifically towards stated objectives has been key, and Farah has engaged the best in the business to help him. His physiologist is Barry Fudge, whose Ph.D thesis looked specifically at the determinants of the success of East African runners. His coach Alberto Salazar also works with Galen Rupp, who finished second to Farah in the 10000metres at London 2012. He noticeably engages with the local culture and athletes as well as taking advantage of the altitude training. He does the important things incredibly well.

Paavo Nurmi

"The Flying Finn" Paavo Nurmi is not only widely considered one of the best long-distance runners of all time, but was part of a dynasty of Finnish runners that dominated international competition in the early part of the 20th Century. Nurmi won nine Olympic gold medals and set 22 official world records at distances between 1,500 metres and 20 kilometres.

Nurmi's training methods and analytical approach have influenced generations of middle and long-distance runners, and indeed his success was a major factor in making running a popular international sport.

He himself was inspired by "Hannes" Kolehmainen the first of this golden generation of Finnish runners. Kolehmainen himself set numerous world records and won 4 Olympic gold medals. Although an outstanding athlete from a young age, Nurmi was always looking for further improvement, usually running with a stopwatch in his hand, and introducing innovations into his training that famously included running whilst holding onto the back of a train. He felt that much of his success, and that of other Finnish runners stemmed from training methods and race tactics that they developed. This included using "speed" sessions effectively, as opposed to just knocking out large volumes of miles. He also described a mental fortitude in himself and his peers, describing a "love of hard work" and a need to fight against obstacles and the odds.

Many of Nurmi's ideas and philosophies including his dedication to training, his use of speed sessions, and his learning from others have stood the test of time, although holding onto the back of a moving train during training runs is no longer recommended!

4) What key lessons can we apply?

Not being from East Africa does not preclude athletes from being world-class middle and long-distance runners. British and Scottish athletes have achieved success on the global stage before, and will do so again. Every runner will have different capabilities and different ambitions, but simple lessons applied consistently can help us enjoy our running and be the best we can.

The hallmarks of the champions are to do the most effective things consistently. In middle and long-distance running, the most important things are to train smart and effectively, to eat the right sort of things, and to allow adequate time for rest and recovery. Doing these three basic things alone will achieve decent success. Once these basics have been taken care of, additional gains can be made by specific training, working on mental preparation, employing injury prevention strategies, going to altitude and the like. But the biggest 'bang for buck' rather than being that fancy pair of new shoes, heart rate monitor, or going to altitude is knowing the basics, and doing them consistently.

Part 7– Who can help me achieve my goals?

You are the single person that will contribute the most to your successes and failures. Having said that, a hallmark of successful runners is involving the right people at the right times. Some runners, such as Mo Farah, may get input from coaches, physiologists, sports massage, physiotherapy, biomechanics, sports medicine and others on a regular basis. For club or recreational runners cost and time mean we tend to seek help more intermittently. This is not to say that you need to involve all these people, but it is intended to provide a basic understanding of who can help can help if required.

1) Coach

Coaches are much underused by runners. Most coaches are highly experienced in advising runners about training regimes, applying tips from other runners, providing motivation, and generally improving your results!

In sport the temptation in general is to spend money on new equipment like golf clubs, or new running shoes but investing a little time and money in getting professional advice on how you can get your best results and best bang for your buck training wise is something that makes a big difference for me, and many other runners.

2) Training partners

In 2011, at one point the 20 fastest marathon times that year were held by Kenyan athletes. Previously other nations in turn had dominated middle and long distance perhaps starting with Finnish athletes that included the great Paavo Nurmi. Running with other people can be the difference between pulling the covers back over your head and going back to sleep and going for that run. It can also drive up standards, especially by running with those slightly quicker than yourself. All in all, training with other people can often help the occasional runner, and the potential world record holder.

3) Friends and family

Having a partner/ family that are supportive of your running helps you achieve more. They can help you get the right amount of sleep, eat the right things, and support your running in many ways. Helping them feel a part of any success you have will keep them happy, and in turn lead to ongoing support and better results.

4) Sports massage

The best friend of the professional athlete, sports massage, has played a part in various cultures for over 3000 years. Sports massage can assist in preventing and treating muscle and other injuries, and is enjoyed by sports people and those with no interest in sport alike.

5) *Physiotherapists*

Physiotherapists are experts in helping you prevent injury by establishing correct movement patterns for you, diagnosing the nature of an injury when it occurs, and guiding rehab/ getting an injury better

6) *Doctors- GP's, and Sports and Exercise Medicine*

Your GP is a great port of call to help with illness and injury. They can often signpost you to an appropriate specialist if needed, and arrange investigations such as x-rays and blood tests.

Sports and Exercise Medicine doctors offer much to recreational and professional athletes. They advise on the prevention and treatment of illness, work closely with physios and others to accurately diagnose and treat injury, and arrange investigations that are needed.

7) *Sports nutrition*

Eating a healthy and balanced diet contributes to performing better. Accredited sports nutritionists can advise on this, and on weight loss strategies.

8) **Strength and conditioning coaches**

They help increase and retain strength, fitness and flexibility aiming to help you perform better and remain injury free.

9) *Sports science*

Physiologists will look closely at how an individual body is performing, and offer input into how this can be improved. Input can focus on training regimes, nutrition, strength and conditioning, and is aimed at improving performance in a scientific way.

10) **Biomechanists**

Biomechanists and performance analysts help develop the most effective and efficient movement patterns to increase performance and help avoid injury. They often use a wide range of tools including force platforms, 3D video analysis, and motion sensors.

11) **Sports psychology**

Mental preparation is equally as key as physical preparation. Sports psychologists aim to help us understand how psychological factors influence performance and can help you develop skills to assist with motivation and performing under pressure as well as dealing with problems as they arise.

12) Past masters

We have a great tradition in Britain of producing good distance runners. In the 1980's there were clusters of centres of excellence in places like Birmingham, Coventry, Gateshead, Aberdeen etc. Many of these runners are still around in our running communities. Talk to them and learn from their experiences, be motivated by what they achieve. Our running clubs are packed with men and women with a passion for running which they will willingly share with new runners.

Conclusions

It is surprisingly easy to put straightforward things in place that will decrease your risk of illness and injury, and boost your chances of performing your best, or at least getting maximum bang for buck. When illness or injury to occur some clever tricks can make sure you are back running as soon as possible. Although we ourselves might not be contenders for Olympic gold, there are lessons we can take from the great athletes to get to where we want to go.

Part 8 – Your information and records

Your personal details and information record

1) Personal details

Name	
Email	
Mobile number	
Coach	
Regular doctor	
Regular physiotherapist	
Emergency contact details	
Event	

2) Medications, allergies and supplements

Medication

Name	Dose	TUE required?

Allergy

Name of substance	Type of reaction	Epipen carried?

Vitamins/ supplements

Name and brand	Dose	Reason for taking

3) *Illness rocord*

Illness type	Dates	Treatment

4) *Injury record*

Injury type	Dates	Treatment, and by who

5) *Vaccinations*

Vaccination	Date	When next required
MMR (mumps, measles, rubella)		
DTP (diphtheria, tetanus, polio)		
Hepatitis A		
Typhoid		
BCG (tuberculosis vaccine)		
Flu (influenza)		

Resources

You may enjoy the following books/ resources that explain aspects of this book in greater details

Lore of Running. Tim Noakes, 4th edition 2002.

Runner's World The Runner's Body. Ross Tucker, Jonathan Dugas, Matt Fitzgerald. 2009

The Chimp Paradox. Steve Peters, 2013.

Elite. The Secret to Exceptional Leadership and Performance. Floyd Woodrow, 2012.

The Sports Gene. David Epstein, 2014.

Train Hard Win Easy. Toby Tanser and John Manners. 1997.

Running Beyond Limits. Andrew Murray, 2011.

Acknowledgements

The expertise and input of colleagues at the SportScotland Institute of Sport, British Athletics, Scottish Rugby Union (in particular Richard Chessor), and Dr Volker Scheer, have helped massively in creating this resource. I can thoroughly recommend reading the resources suggested, as I refer to these texts most days to learn a little bit more.

Thanks to George Winter, Fraser Clyne, and Colin McPhail for their excellent insights, and assistance in proof reading and editing.